Amazing
Crocodiles
& Reptiles

WRITTEN BY
MARY LING

PHOTOGRAPHED BY
JERRY YOUNG

Stoddart

Conceived and produced by
Dorling Kindersley Limited

Project editor Christine Webb
Art editor Toni Rann
Senior art editor Jacquie Gulliver
Production Louise Barratt

Illustrations by Colin Woolf, Julie Anderson,
and John Hutchinson
Animals supplied by Trevor Smith's Animal World
and Cotswold Wildlife Park
Editorial consultants The staff of the Natural History Museum, London

Published in Canada in 1991 by Stoddart Publishing Co. Limited
34 Lesmill Road, Toronto, Canada M3B 2T6
Published in Great Britain in 1991 by Dorling Kindersley Limited
9 Henrietta Street, London, England WC2E 8PS

Canadian Cataloguing in Publication Data
Ling, Mary
Amazing crocodiles and reptiles
(Amazing worlds)
ISBN 0-7737-2474-5
1. Crocodiles - Juvenile literature. 2. Reptiles - Juvenile
literature. I. Young, Jerry. II. Title. III. Series.
QL666.C9L36 1991   j597.9   C90-095672-0

Color reproduction by Colourscan, Singapore
Typeset by Windsorgraphics, Ringwood, Hampshire
Printed in Italy by A. Mondadori Editore, Verona

Contents

What is a reptile?

Reptiles are the last living relatives of the dinosaurs. For one hundred million years, reptiles were masters of the earth.

Family tree
What do snakes, lizards, crocodilians (that's crocodiles, alligators, gavials, and caimans) the turtle family, and the tuatara have in common? They're all reptiles, that's what.

Heat up, cool down
Reptiles are cold-blooded, which means they are the same temperature as the air or water around them. When they're cold, they bask in the sun, and when they get too hot, they pick a shady spot to cool down in.

Most reptiles swing their backs from side to side when they walk

Like most reptiles, crocodiles have short legs

No sweat

Basking in the sun all day would make you hot and sticky – and very thirsty. But reptiles have scaly, watertight skin from head to toe, so their bodies don't dry out.

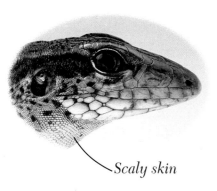
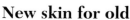
Scaly skin

Egg layers

Nearly all reptiles lay eggs. Most babies hatch when they are ready, but the Nile crocodile gently cracks the eggs open with her teeth if she thinks they're taking too long.

There is no hair on the dry, scaly skin

New skin for old

All reptiles shed their skin. Some snakes shuffle out of theirs in one try. But lizards lose their skin bit by bit. Sometimes they even tug off the stubborn pieces with their teeth!

Crocodiles lift their bodies off the ground when they walk

Nifty movers

This dwarf crocodile lives in the forests of West Africa. It might look clumsy when it's walking, but it moves just fine once it's spied a tasty frog or fish!

The incredible hunter

With powerful jaws studded with teeth, and skin like a suit of armor, the Nile crocodile can overpower almost any animal it chooses.

Death roll

Crocodiles lunge out of the water as quick as a flash and clamp their victims with power-packed jaws. They spin and twist in the water to tear off bite-sized chunks of meat. Then they swallow the pieces of meat – whole.

Fish eaters

Gavials have long, slim jaws with a hundred razor-sharp teeth. A quick sideways sweep of the head through the water traps a passing fish. Then, with one toss of the head, it's down the hatch.

Crocodiles only have about 50 meals a year

The scales on the Nile crocodile's tail form a spiky ridge

Crocodiles can't stick their tongues out

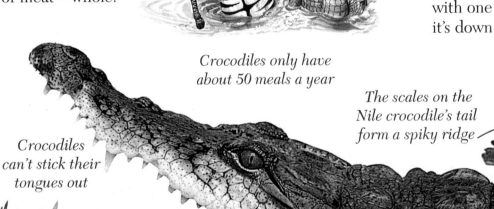

Sun seekers

Nile crocodiles can be found basking on riverbanks all over tropical Africa. At 4 feet long, this croc still has a long way to go before it catches up with the longest Nile crocodile ever found – which measured nearly 20 feet!

Diners' club
Crocodiles are not greedy. As many as 30 or 40 may join in a zebra feast, helping one another tear off morsels of meat.

The crocodile god
The ancient Egyptians feared and worshipped Nile crocodiles so much that their god of power, Sobek, had a crocodile's head.

Man-made meal
For some crocodiles, humans are on the menu. So take care when you step on a floating log. It may be a lurking croc waiting to snap you up.

Living toothpick
When they get hot, crocodiles rest with their mouths gaping open. They don't seem to mind when birds such as plovers pick leftover food from between their teeth.

Living in a box

The tortoise is a moving fortress. It has such a heavy shell to carry around that it can't run, jump, or swim. That's why it lives only on land.

Safe as houses

A tortoise's shell protects its whole body. The shell is made of bone and covered with a layer of tough scales made from the same stuff as your fingernails. The part that covers the back is joined to the tortoise's spine and ribs.

Little and large

There are about 40 different kinds of tortoise. Some are only a few inches long, but others measure well over 3 feet.

Home and away

When danger threatens, most tortoises and turtles pull their head and legs into their shells. But some, like this snake-necked turtle, just wind their long necks around and tuck their heads in.

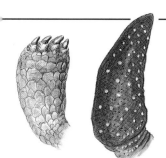

Land   *Sea*   *Fresh water*

No teeth!

Tortoises and turtles do not have teeth. Instead, their jaws have razor-sharp edges that can snip twigs and tear flesh.

Feet apart

Plodding tortoises have elephant-like feet. Sea turtles have front flippers like paddles. And turtles and terrapins, which live in fresh and salty water, have webbed feet.

Groovy shells

Tortoises from the Galapagos Islands have tailor-made shells. On lush green islands, the tortoises have gently curving shells that don't get in the way when they're eating. But on islands where food is high up a branch, their shells have grooves behind the neck for easier high-rise eating.

Red-legged tortoise

This tortoise (left) roams the humid forests of South America. At full size, its shell can be as long as 20 inches – that's quite a handful!

Slithering snakes

Snakes manage very well without legs. Some climb trees, some slither around on the ground, and others are expert swimmers. A few snakes can even glide through the air.

Snakes move from branch to branch by stretching out, head first

Markings look like piano keys

Deadly fangs

Some snakes are poisonous. When they want a bite to eat, they sink their sharp fangs into their victim and pump in a deadly poison. Then the feast begins.

Snake eyes

Snakes have no eyelids. Instead, see-through scales cover their eyes like eyeglasses. When a snake sheds its skin, it gets new glasses too.

Hundred flower rat snake

This snake (below) can be found slinking along branches in the bamboo forests of southern China. One of its favorite meals is – you guessed it – rats!

Born swimmers

The yellow-bellied sea snake spends all its life in the water. It uses its flat tail like a paddle to zoom around at top speed.

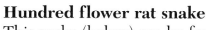

Supper sense

Many snakes and lizards don't smell with their noses like we do. They flick their tongues in and out to "taste" the air for a passing meal. Then the scent is picked up by a special smelling organ in the mouth.

Magnificent movers

Some snakes move in special ways. The sidewinder (right) tiptoes across the American desert in a zigzag dance, keeping its belly off the hot sand.

Big mouth

Having a snake's jaws would make mealtime a lot more simple. A snake can open its jaws so wide that it can swallow a meal much bigger than its head – whole.

Amazing alligators

Next time you come across a crocodilian with its mouth closed, check its teeth. If the fourth tooth on the bottom pokes out, then it's a crocodile. But if all its bottom teeth are tucked in, then it's an alligator, like this one.

Caiman

Alligator

Watch out for snouts
The snout is a crocodilian's greatest weapon. Gavials have long, narrow jaws for catching fish. Alligators have broad, stout snouts. Crocodiles and caimans have slimmer, medium-sized jaws.

An alligator can grow forty or fifty new sets of teeth in a lifetime

Crocodile

Gavial

Smash
Alligators and crocodiles can't chew food before they swallow it, as their teeth are only good for grabbing and tearing. So they swallow stones to help smash up the food they've eaten.

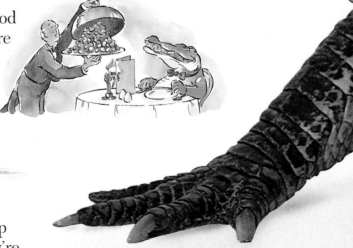

Belly full
Stones also stop them from bobbing up and giving themselves away when they're stalking prey in the water.

What a racket!
A big alligator's bellow is something to hear. It sounds like a huge, noisy engine. And when one alligator gets going, its neighbors soon join in.

Record breaker
You'd have trouble getting the longest American alligator ever found into your bedroom *and* closing the door behind you. It was 19 feet long.

American alligator
Next time you're in the swamps of Florida, watch for this alligator. If it's resting with its mouth wide open, don't worry – it's just feeling hot and trying to cool down.

Strange shapes and shells

Tall, strong shells make safe homes on land. In the water, light, slim shells work best. But wherever turtles live, they have ways of staying extra safe.

Leather shell

The leatherback is the largest sea turtle around. It can weigh as much as 2,000 pounds. Instead of a heavy shell and scales, it has tiny bony plates under its leathery skin.

Fold-away neck

This snake-necked turtle lives in rivers in Australia. It hunts fish, snails, and shrimp among rocks with the help of its hoselike neck, which is as long as its body.

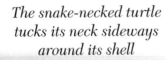

The snake-necked turtle tucks its neck sideways around its shell

Prickly turtle?

When it is born, the spiny forest turtle's shell is very soft. The shell's jagged edge gives the young turtle extra protection while it waits for its armor to toughen up.

Stinkpots

These little turtles live in North America. When birds try to pick them up, the turtles give off a disgusting smell. That's why they're called stinkpots.

Crunch proof

Sharing the river with alligators must be nerve-racking. So the Florida red-bellied turtle has a strong, high shell to protect itself from the alligators' deadly crunching jaws.

Flat as a ...

This is one pancake you won't want to eat. The African pancake tortoise has a flat shell. When danger threatens, it can run very fast (for a tortoise) and squeeze into tiny spaces where enemies can't reach.

Webbed feet, just right for fast river swimming

Snorkeling turtle

The matamata turtle of Brazil sits on the river-bed waiting for supper to swim by. Using its long, stretchy neck, it pokes its nostrils out of the water to take a breath, without having to move and frighten the fish.

Useful lizard

Lizards live in every part of the world except in deepest, coldest Antarctica. Some of them make wonderful house guests – they run around lapping up flies and mosquitoes.

Ancient tuatara
It may look like a lizard but, in the family of reptiles, the tuatara is in a group of its own. In the time of the dinosaurs, its relatives lived all over the world. Now they live only in parts of New Zealand.

Early riser
Most geckos prefer the night life, but the Madagascar day gecko wakes up in the day. It lives in trees in the forests of Madagascar, eating small insects and fruit. For a special treat, it likes a lick of honey.

Geckos lick their eyeballs to keep them clean

Prickly lizard
When it senses danger, the armadillo lizard just rolls up into a hoop, tucks its tail in its mouth, and sits tight. Its tough, prickly spikes help to shield its belly, the only soft part of its body.

Shattered
The Pallas's glass snake (right) is a lizard with no legs and a special "snap-off" tail. If it is caught, its tail breaks up into tiny wriggling pieces while the rest of it makes a quick getaway.

Don't step on my tail
The Oriental long-tailed lizard has an unusual way of getting around. It throws itself from stalk to stalk in its grassy meadow home, keeping balance with its amazingly long tail.

Lash out
When the Gould's monitor lizard is threatened, it hisses loudly and rears up on its back legs to frighten its attacker.

Skin changes
Chameleons change color depending on the heat and the sun. This chameleon has a leafy pattern on its skin from sunbathing on a leafy branch. The skin that was in the shade hasn't changed color.

Slow movers

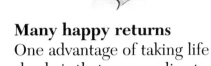

Imagine carrying your home around on your back. You wouldn't win many races.

Head for danger
The big-headed turtle can't tuck its head into its shell when it's in danger – the head doesn't fit. But its long tail helps it clamber over rocks and plants for a quick getaway.

Many happy returns
One advantage of taking life slowly is that you can live to a ripe old age. One male Marion's tortoise lived to be 152! That's a lot of candles on a birthday cake.

Powerful paddles
Sea turtles look exhausted crawling on land, but they glide gracefully in water. They can speed along at up to 40 miles per hour if need be, flapping their powerful flippers like wings.

Thick shell under belly protects against rough stones and twigs

The hare and the tortoise

In an old story, a hare and a tortoise had a race. The hare got so far ahead that he took a nap. When he woke up, he was too late. The tortoise had plodded steadily all the way and won the race!

House guests

The gopher tortoise lives in a deep tunnel, which it shares with gopher frogs and mice. To keep hungry snakes out, the tortoise defends its home by parking itself in the doorway.

Slow coach

The beautiful starred tortoise (left) plods along at about 650 feet per hour. If it played football, it would take half an hour to get from one end of the field to the other.

This tortoise drags itself along using its strong front legs

Crocodiles in water

Crocodiles live at the water's edge where they enjoy the best of both worlds: land and water. On land, they move clumsily. But in the water, they are elegant, powerful swimmers.

See through
When we dive underwater, we have to wear goggles to protect our eyes. Crocs have three eyelids – two where eyelids usually are and a third, see-through lid which moves across from side to side for safe underwater sight.

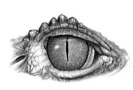

The first croc?
An old story tells of a poor man named Ginja who caught on fire. He rushed into the river to put the fire out. But the heat had blistered his skin. Ginja became the first crocodile.

Crocodiles can hold their breath for more than an hour

Diving equipment
Catching and swallowing prey underwater could be tricky if crocodiles gulped too much water. A muscular flap which closes off the mouth from the breathing tubes stops them from choking.

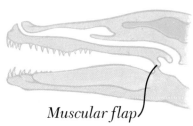

Muscular flap

Modern caiman
The spectacled caiman of South America has learned to live in a modern world. It has discovered that man-made dams and cattle ponds make comfortable homes.

A rug of mud
Mud makes a wonderful blanket –
cools you if you're hot, warms you
if you're feeling chilly. It also makes
you a less inviting meal
for annoying insects.

Crocodile tears
People used to think
that crocodiles shed
tears when they ate their
victims. Now we know
that they're just getting
rid of all the salt they've
swallowed in the water!

A strong tail
Crocs tuck their legs in and
use their tails to push them
through the water. Their tails
are so strong and
powerful that some
crocodiles have
been known to
"tail-walk."

Eat or be eaten

Being a slow mover can be a problem if you don't like plants or snails or worms for dinner. Some turtles have clever ways of snaring meals that go whizzing by.

Vacuum eater

The matamata stands so still on the muddy riverbed that its lumpy shell looks like a rock. When fish swim near, it suddenly opens its enormous mouth. In rushes the water – and the fish, too.

Living larder

The first explorers in the Galapagos Islands found the tortoises there very useful. They trapped them and ate them on the voyage home. Until then the tortoises had had no enemies.

Turtle treats

Some baby turtles don't even get to taste their first meal. As newly hatched green turtles run down the beach toward the sea for their first swim, hungry sea gulls swoop down and snatch up the unlucky ones.

Open wide

The alligator snapping turtle sits quietly on the riverbed with its mouth wide open, waiting for its next meal to swim by. On its tongue is a bright pink growth that looks just like a wiggling worm.

Crunch

When a curious fish comes too close, sharp jaws slam shut on it.

Watch-dog turtles

Loggerhead turtles crush crabs and clams in their vicious jaws. Their bite is so savage that the Sri Lankans call them dog turtles.

The snapping turtle's massive head and arms can't fit into its shell

Snapped up

If you ever come across a snapping turtle, keep your fingers well away. It will bite just about anything that comes too close to its powerful beak.

Hatching out

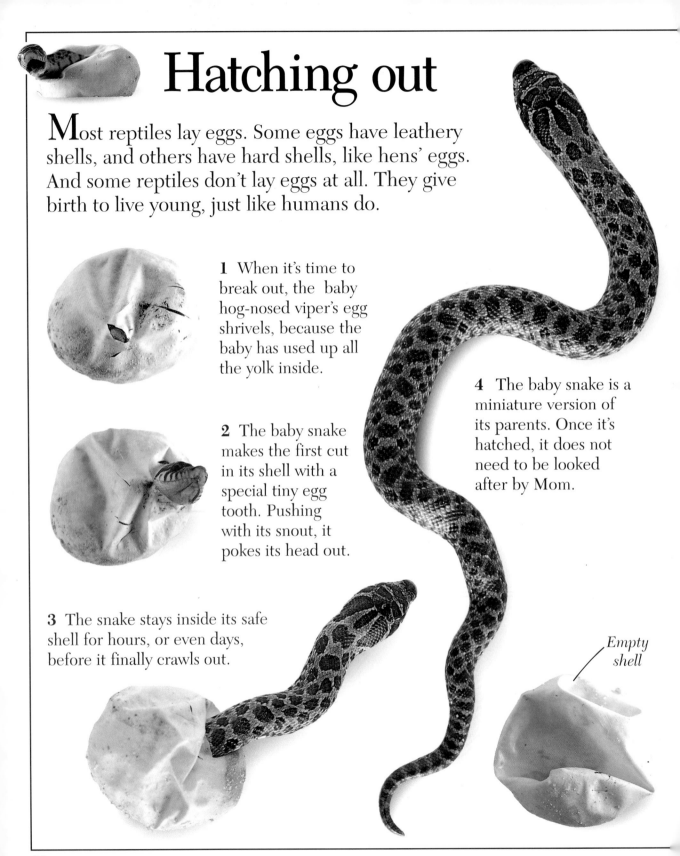

Most reptiles lay eggs. Some eggs have leathery shells, and others have hard shells, like hens' eggs. And some reptiles don't lay eggs at all. They give birth to live young, just like humans do.

1 When it's time to break out, the baby hog-nosed viper's egg shrivels, because the baby has used up all the yolk inside.

2 The baby snake makes the first cut in its shell with a special tiny egg tooth. Pushing with its snout, it pokes its head out.

4 The baby snake is a miniature version of its parents. Once it's hatched, it does not need to be looked after by Mom.

3 The snake stays inside its safe shell for hours, or even days, before it finally crawls out.

Empty shell

Long wait

The estuarine crocodile makes a nest of rotting plants to keep its eggs warm. After the eggs are laid, the mother guards them until they hatch.

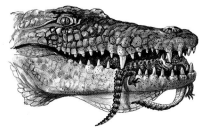

Caring parents

When baby crocodiles hatch, their mother gently gathers as many as she can into her mouth and places them in a nursery pool.

Egg snatchers

During the nesting season, reptile parents watch out for monitor lizards, whose favorite meal is a batch of fresh reptile eggs.

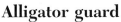

Alligator guard

The Florida red-bellied turtle lays her eggs in an alligator's nest. The reward for risking her life to do this is a warm place for her eggs and a free egg sitter.

So many eggs

This green turtle's mother travels a very long way to lay her eggs on the same beach every year. And of the 2,000 eggs she lays in her lifetime, only three will become adults.